The 2025 Entrepreneur

Business Ideas for a Changing World

Ghazwan Alemara

Contents

Introduction

What does it take to thrive in a world that never stops changing? As technology continues to reshape industries, sustainability becomes a driving force in consumer behavior, and the future of work transforms how we live and operate, the entrepreneurial landscape is evolving at an unprecedented pace. For aspiring business leaders, staying ahead of these shifts isn't just a choice, it's the key to survival and success.

This book is your essential guide to navigating the business world of tomorrow. It's designed to help you understand the transformative trends shaping 2025 and equip you with the tools to turn challenges into opportunities. Whether you're an aspiring entrepreneur taking your first steps, a seasoned business owner looking to adapt, or someone seeking innovative ideas to redefine your path, this book will empower you to take control of your future.

The business world is no longer bound by traditional methods and expectations. Technology, including artificial intelligence, blockchain, and the Internet of Things, is driving unprecedented innovation and efficiency. Sustainability is no longer just a trend; it's a necessity for businesses aiming to stay relevant and build lasting consumer trust. The rise of remote work and digital collaboration has transformed how businesses operate, offering new flexibility and opportunities to engage with global talent.

This book explores these dynamics in detail, offering actionable insights to help you succeed in this new era.

You'll discover how to align your strengths with market demands, identify low-investment opportunities, and leverage cutting-edge technologies to create value. From sustainable and socially conscious businesses to tech-driven and brick-and-mortar ventures, this book presents a comprehensive roadmap for entrepreneurs ready to adapt to the realities of a rapidly changing world. You'll also explore real-life examples of successful businesses that have embraced change, overcome challenges, and emerged as leaders in their fields.

Every chapter is crafted to guide you through key aspects of building a thriving business. You'll learn how to create a solid business plan, find and engage your target audience, and build a strong brand that resonates with modern consumers. With practical advice on leveraging online tools, embracing digital transformation, and adapting to future trends, this book provides the knowledge and strategies you need to stay competitive.

But this book isn't just about strategies and trends, it's about the mindset needed to embrace change, take risks, and innovate. The future belongs to those who are ready to challenge norms, learn continuously, and turn disruption into opportunity. With the insights and guidance offered here, you'll not only be prepared to face the challenges of 2025 but also to seize the opportunities that come with them.

The journey ahead is both exciting and demanding. The business landscape of the future will test your adaptability, resilience, and creativity. This book will be your companion, offering clarity, inspiration, and practical tools to help you navigate the unknown with confidence. So, let's dive in and explore the possibilities that lie ahead. Together, we'll chart a course toward success in a world that rewards visionaries who dare to dream and act boldly. The future is waiting, are you ready to take the leap?

Chapter 1

The Business Landscape in 2025

Overview of Current Trends

In the ever-evolving landscape of business, staying abreast of current trends is paramount for success. Several transformative trends are reshaping industries worldwide, fundamentally altering the way businesses operate, innovate, and compete. In this section, we embark on a deep dive into three key trends driving change in the business landscape: the Remote Work Revolution, Sustainability Initiatives, and Technological Advancements.

Remote Work Revolution:

The Remote Work Revolution has emerged as one of the most consequential shifts in the modern workplace, propelled by advancements in technology, changing attitudes towards work-life balance, and the global response to the COVID-19 pandemic. In 2024, remote work has transitioned from a temporary necessity to a permanent fixture, with organizations of all sizes embracing flexible work arrangements and distributed teams.

One of the defining features of the Remote Work Revolution is the widespread adoption of digital collaboration tools, enabling seamless communication, project management, and virtual meetings across geographies. Platforms like Zoom, Slack, and Microsoft Teams have become indispensable tools for remote teams, fostering a sense of connectivity and collaboration in a virtual environment.

Moreover, the Remote Work Revolution has sparked a reevaluation of traditional office spaces, with many companies opting for hybrid work models that combine remote and in-person work. This shift has profound implications for real estate markets, urban planning, and the future of work, as businesses seek to balance the benefits of remote work with the importance of physical presence and collaboration.

From a workforce perspective, remote work has democratized access to job opportunities, enabling individuals to work from anywhere and pursue flexible careers that align with their lifestyle preferences. This trend has spurred the rise of digital nomadism, with remote workers embracing a nomadic lifestyle, traveling the world while maintaining their professional commitments.

However, the Remote Work Revolution also presents unique challenges, including the need for robust cybersecurity measures to protect remote work environments, the importance of maintaining work-life balance in an always-on digital world, and the potential for feelings of isolation and burnout among remote workers.

Despite these challenges, the Remote Work Revolution represents a paradigm shift in the way businesses approach work, offering opportunities for increased productivity, cost savings, and talent acquisition on a global scale. As we navigate through 2025 and beyond, businesses must adapt to this new reality, embracing remote work as a catalyst for innovation, collaboration, and growth.

Sustainability Initiatives:

Sustainability Initiatives have emerged as a driving force behind consumer behavior, corporate strategy, and regulatory frameworks, as businesses worldwide grapple with the urgent need to address environmental and social challenges. From climate change mitigation to resource conservation and social responsibility, sustainability has become a central pillar of business strategy, guiding decision-making and shaping corporate identity.

One of the most notable trends in sustainability is the growing demand for eco-friendly products and services, driven by increased consumer awareness of environmental issues and the desire to minimize ecological footprints. In response, businesses are innovating new sustainable products, incorporating recycled materials, reducing waste, and embracing circular economy principles to create value while minimizing environmental impact.

Moreover, Sustainability Initiatives are driving transparency and accountability across supply chains, as consumers and stakeholders demand greater visibility into the environmental and social practices of companies. From fair trade certifications to carbon footprint tracking, businesses are leveraging technology to track and report on their sustainability efforts, building trust and credibility with consumers and investors.

The shift towards sustainability also extends to corporate governance and social responsibility, as businesses recognize the importance of aligning their operations with broader societal values and priorities. From diversity and inclusion initiatives to community engagement and philanthropy, companies are embracing a holistic approach to corporate citizenship, seeking to create positive social impact while delivering value to shareholders.

However, implementing Sustainability Initiatives is not without its challenges, including the need for significant investments in sustainable infrastructure, supply chain optimization, and stakeholder engagement. Moreover, businesses must navigate complex regulatory frameworks and market dynamics, balancing short-term financial pressures with long-term sustainability goals.

Despite these challenges, Sustainability Initiatives present significant opportunities for businesses to drive innovation, differentiate their brands, and create shared value for society and the environment. Businesses must embrace sustainability as a strategic imperative, integrating environmental and social considerations into their core business practices to thrive in a rapidly evolving market landscape.

Technological Advancements:

Technological Advancements continue to revolutionize industries and redefine the way businesses operate, innovate, and compete. In 2025, we stand on the cusp of a new era of technological innovation, driven by breakthroughs in artificial intelligence, machine learning, blockchain, and the Internet of Things.

One of the most transformative trends in technology is the rise of artificial intelligence (AI) and machine learning, enabling businesses to automate processes, analyze vast amounts of data, and uncover actionable insights in real-time. From predictive analytics and personalized recommendations to autonomous systems and natural language processing, AI is revolutionizing industries ranging from healthcare and finance to retail and manufacturing.

Moreover, blockchain technology is disrupting traditional business models and unlocking new possibilities for secure, transparent, and decentralized transactions. From cryptocurrency and smart contracts to supply chain management and digital identity verification, blockchain has the potential to revolutionize industries and reshape the future of commerce.

The Internet of Things (IoT) is another key trend driving technological innovation, connecting billions of devices and enabling seamless communication and data exchange across networks. From smart homes and wearable devices to connected cars and industrial sensors, IoT is transforming industries, optimizing operations, and enhancing the customer experience in unprecedented ways.

However, as businesses embrace Technological Advancements, they must also grapple with ethical considerations, privacy concerns, and the potential for unintended consequences. From algorithmic bias and data privacy breaches to cybersecurity threats and job displacement, businesses must navigate complex ethical and regulatory frameworks to ensure that technology is used responsibly and ethically.

Despite these challenges, Technological Advancements present unparalleled opportunities for businesses to innovate, disrupt industries, and unlock new revenue streams. Businesses must embrace technology as a strategic enabler, leveraging AI, blockchain, IoT, and other emerging technologies to drive growth, enhance competitiveness, and create value for customers and stakeholders alike.

The business landscape in 2025 is defined by transformative trends that are reshaping industries, challenging traditional business models, and unlocking new opportunities for innovation and growth. From the Remote Work Revolution and Sustainability Initiatives to Technological Advancements, businesses must adapt to this new reality, embracing change as a catalyst for progress and reinvention in a dynamic and ever-evolving marketplace.

The Evolution of Business: Adapting to Change

Adaptation is the key to survival. It becomes evident that businesses are navigating a landscape characterized by rapid change, disruptive forces, and unprecedented challenges. In this section, we explore the evolution of business in response to shifting market dynamics, technological advancements, and changing consumer preferences.

Adapting to Digital Transformation:

One of the most significant trends shaping the evolution of business is the ongoing process of digital transformation. From the proliferation of e-commerce to the adoption of cloud computing and big data analytics, businesses are harnessing digital technologies to streamline operations, enhance customer experiences, and drive innovation.

In response to the COVID-19 pandemic, digital transformation has accelerated across industries, as businesses seek to adapt to remote work, online commerce, and virtual collaboration. Organizations that were once hesitant to embrace digital technologies have been forced to pivot quickly, digitizing operations, and embracing digital-first strategies to remain competitive in a rapidly evolving marketplace.

Moreover, digital transformation has blurred the lines between industries, enabling new business models, and reshaping traditional value chains. From digital disruptors challenging incumbents in sectors like finance, healthcare, and transportation to legacy companies embracing technology to reinvent themselves, the digital revolution is reshaping the competitive landscape in profound ways.

However, digital transformation is not without its challenges. Businesses must navigate complex technological ecosystems, address cybersecurity threats, and bridge the digital divide to ensure that all stakeholders can participate in the digital economy. Moreover, organizations must cultivate a culture of innovation and adaptability to thrive in an environment characterized by constant change and disruption.

Embracing Agile Methodologies:

In the face of uncertainty and volatility, businesses are increasingly embracing agile methodologies to adapt quickly to changing market conditions, customer preferences, and technological advancements. Agile methodologies, rooted in principles of flexibility, collaboration, and iterative development, enable organizations to respond rapidly to emerging opportunities and challenges, delivering value to customers more efficiently and effectively.

One of the hallmarks of agile methodologies is cross-functional teams, composed of individuals with diverse skills and perspectives who collaborate closely to solve problems and deliver results. By breaking down silos and fostering collaboration across departments, agile teams can accelerate decision-making, reduce time to market, and drive innovation in a fast-paced and competitive environment.

Moreover, agile methodologies prioritize customer feedback and iteration, enabling businesses to test hypotheses, gather data, and refine their strategies based on real-world insights. By embracing a mindset of continuous improvement and experimentation, organizations can adapt quickly to changing market dynamics, pivot when necessary, and stay ahead of the curve in a rapidly evolving marketplace.

However, implementing agile methodologies requires a cultural shift within organizations, as well as investment in training, infrastructure, and processes to support agile ways of working. Moreover, businesses must strike a balance between agility and stability, ensuring that they can respond quickly to change without sacrificing reliability, quality, or compliance.

Navigating Regulatory Complexity:

In an increasingly interconnected and regulated global economy, businesses must navigate a complex web of regulatory frameworks, compliance requirements, and geopolitical risks. From data privacy regulations like the GDPR and CCPA to trade policies, tax laws, and environmental regulations, compliance is a critical consideration for businesses operating across borders and industries.

Moreover, the regulatory landscape is constantly evolving, as governments respond to emerging threats, technological advancements, and shifting societal values. Businesses must stay abreast of regulatory changes, monitor compliance requirements, and adapt their strategies and operations accordingly to mitigate risks and ensure legal and ethical conduct.

However, compliance is not just a legal obligation—it is also a strategic imperative. By adopting a proactive approach to compliance, businesses can build trust with customers, investors, and other stakeholders, differentiate themselves from competitors, and create a culture of integrity and accountability that drives long-term success.

Moreover, businesses must navigate geopolitical risks, including trade tensions, political instability, and social unrest, which can impact supply chains, operations, and market access. By monitoring geopolitical developments, diversifying supply chains, and building resilience into their operations, businesses can mitigate risks and seize opportunities in an uncertain world.

The evolution of business in 2025 is characterized by adaptation to change, as organizations embrace digital transformation, agile methodologies, and regulatory compliance to thrive in a rapidly evolving marketplace. By embracing agility, innovation, and integrity, businesses can navigate uncertainty, seize opportunities, and build a resilient foundation for long-term success in the dynamic landscape of the 21st century.

Chapter 2

Identifying Your Strengths & Interests

Assessing Your Skills

In the journey of entrepreneurship, understanding one's own strengths and capabilities is paramount. This section serves as a foundational step, guiding readers to recognize and leverage their unique talents, experiences, and proficiencies in pursuit of entrepreneurial endeavors.

Understanding Transferable Skills:

At the heart of assessing one's skills lies the concept of transferable skills—those abilities and competencies that can be applied across various domains and contexts. Whether gained through professional experiences, academic pursuits, or personal interests, transferable skills serve as versatile assets that can empower individuals to excel in diverse roles and industries.

Identifying transferable skills begins with self-reflection and introspection. Readers are encouraged to assess their past experiences, accomplishments, and challenges, identifying key skills that have contributed to their success or growth. From communication and problem-solving to leadership and adaptability, transferable skills encompass a broad spectrum of competencies that shape one's professional journey.

Moreover, recognizing transferable skills involves soliciting feedback from peers, mentors, and colleagues, gaining valuable insights into strengths and areas for development. Through constructive feedback and self-assessment exercises, readers can gain a deeper understanding of their unique skill set, identifying areas of expertise to leverage and areas for growth to cultivate.

Once identified, transferable skills serve as a foundation for exploring potential business opportunities, aligning personal strengths with market demands and emerging trends. By leveraging transferable skills, aspiring entrepreneurs can capitalize on their core competencies, positioning themselves for success in competitive and dynamic business landscapes.

Exploring Passion and Proficiency:

In addition to assessing transferable skills, understanding one's passions and interests is equally crucial in the journey of entrepreneurship. The intersection of passion and proficiency serves as a guiding compass, steering individuals towards business ventures that align with their personal values, interests, and aspirations.

Exploring passions begins with introspection and self-awareness, prompting readers to reflect on activities, hobbies, and experiences that ignite genuine enthusiasm and fulfillment. Whether it's a love for technology, a passion for sustainability, or a fascination with creative expression, identifying passions provides valuable insight into potential business ventures that resonate on a personal level.

Furthermore, exploring proficiency involves evaluating areas of expertise, knowledge, and skills that one has developed through formal education, professional experiences, or independent pursuits. By assessing proficiency in specific domains, individuals can identify niche opportunities where their expertise can create value and differentiation in the marketplace.

However, the convergence of passion and proficiency is not always straightforward. Readers are encouraged to explore intersections between their passions and proficiencies, identifying areas of overlap and alignment that hold the greatest potential for entrepreneurial success. Whether it's leveraging technical expertise to address environmental challenges or combining artistic talents with digital innovation, the synergy between passion and proficiency serves as a catalyst for innovative business ideas.

Moreover, exploring passion and proficiency involves embracing a growth mindset, recognizing that skills can be developed and passions can evolve over time. By remaining open to new experiences, learning opportunities, and feedback, aspiring entrepreneurs can continually refine their understanding of their strengths and interests, paving the way for meaningful and fulfilling business ventures.

Harnessing Skills for Entrepreneurial Success:

As readers embark on the journey of entrepreneurship, harnessing their assessed skills becomes essential for navigating challenges, seizing opportunities, and achieving sustainable success. Whether launching a startup, pursuing freelance ventures, or exploring new business opportunities, leveraging skills effectively can empower individuals to overcome obstacles and thrive in competitive markets.

One key aspect of harnessing skills for entrepreneurial success involves strategic positioning and differentiation. By leveraging their unique strengths and competencies, entrepreneurs can carve out niche markets, differentiate their offerings, and create value propositions that resonate with target audiences. Whether it's offering specialized services, developing innovative solutions, or delivering exceptional customer experiences, harnessing skills strategically is essential for gaining a competitive edge in crowded marketplaces.

Moreover, harnessing skills for entrepreneurial success involves continuous learning and skill development. As business landscapes evolve and market dynamics shift, entrepreneurs must remain agile and adaptable, continuously honing their skills, staying abreast of industry trends, and embracing lifelong learning opportunities. By investing in skill development and staying ahead of the curve, entrepreneurs can position themselves for long-term growth and sustainability in dynamic and competitive environments.

Furthermore, harnessing skills for entrepreneurial success involves building a strong support network and leveraging complementary talents. Collaborating with partners, mentors, advisors, and fellow entrepreneurs can provide valuable insights, resources, and support, enabling individuals to overcome challenges, capitalize on opportunities, and achieve collective goals. By surrounding themselves with a diverse and supportive network, entrepreneurs can leverage collective expertise and experience, accelerating their journey towards entrepreneurial success.

Assessing one's skills is a foundational step in the entrepreneurial journey, guiding individuals to recognize their strengths, interests, and potential for success in business ventures. By understanding transferable skills, exploring passions and proficiencies, and harnessing skills strategically, aspiring entrepreneurs can position themselves for success in dynamic and competitive business landscapes, unlocking their full potential as innovative leaders and change-makers in the global marketplace.

Understanding Your Interests

Understanding your interests is a crucial aspect of identifying viable business opportunities and aligning your entrepreneurial pursuits with your personal passions and values. In this section, we delve into the significance of exploring and understanding your interests in the context of entrepreneurial endeavors. By gaining clarity on what truly excites and motivates you, you can embark on a path that not only brings financial success but also fulfillment and satisfaction.

Defining Personal Values and Passions:

At the core of understanding your interests lies the exploration of your personal values and passions. Your values are the guiding principles that define what is important to you, shaping your decisions, actions, and priorities. By identifying your values, you gain insight into the underlying motivations and aspirations that drive your entrepreneurial ambitions.

Reflect on the principles and ideals that resonate with you on a deep level. Are you passionate about environmental sustainability, social justice, innovation, or personal development? Consider the causes, issues, or areas of impact that ignite a sense of purpose and fulfillment within you. These are the clues that can lead you towards business opportunities that align with your values and passions.

Furthermore, consider your hobbies, interests, and activities that bring you joy and satisfaction outside of work. Whether it's a love for outdoor adventures, a passion for cooking, or a fascination with technology, these personal interests can serve as valuable indicators of potential business avenues that allow you to combine passion with profession.

Exploring Market Gaps and Opportunities:

Once you have identified your personal values and passions, the next step is to explore how they intersect with market gaps and opportunities. Entrepreneurial success often hinges on the ability to identify unmet needs, underserved markets, or emerging trends that align with your interests and expertise.

Conduct market research to identify areas where your passions and skills can address existing challenges or capitalize on emerging opportunities. Look for gaps in the market where your unique perspective, knowledge, or approach can provide innovative solutions or create value for customers.

For example, if you are passionate about sustainability and have expertise in product design, you may explore opportunities to create eco-friendly alternatives to existing products or services. Similarly, if you are passionate about health and wellness and have a background in nutrition, you may consider launching a wellness coaching business or developing a line of healthy food products.

By aligning your interests with market needs and opportunities, you not only increase the likelihood of success but also ensure that your entrepreneurial endeavors are driven by genuine passion and purpose.

Assessing Personal Skills and Competencies:

In addition to understanding your interests and values, it is essential to assess your personal skills, strengths, and competencies. Your skills and expertise play a crucial role in determining the feasibility and viability of potential business ideas, as well as your ability to execute them successfully.

Take inventory of your professional experience, education, training, and skills acquired through previous roles or projects. Identify your areas of expertise, strengths, and competencies that can be leveraged to create value in the marketplace. Whether it's technical skills, creative abilities, interpersonal strengths, or leadership qualities, understanding your capabilities is essential for identifying entrepreneurial opportunities that align with your strengths.

Moreover, consider your willingness and capacity to acquire new skills or knowledge relevant to your entrepreneurial pursuits. Continuous learning and skill development are essential for staying relevant and competitive in today's fast-paced business environment. Be open to acquiring new skills, seeking out mentors or advisors, and investing in your personal and professional growth to enhance your entrepreneurial success.

Exploring Potential Business Ideas:

Armed with a deeper understanding of your interests, values, and skills, it's time to explore potential business ideas that align with your entrepreneurial aspirations. Brainstorm a range of ideas based on your passions, market insights, and personal strengths, considering both traditional and innovative approaches to addressing market needs or opportunities.

Evaluate each business idea based on criteria such as market demand, feasibility, scalability, and alignment with your values and long-term goals. Consider how each idea leverages your unique strengths and interests, as well as its potential for impact, profitability, and sustainability.

Narrow down your list of potential business ideas to those that resonate most strongly with you, align with your values and passions, and have the greatest potential for success. Remember that entrepreneurship is a journey of exploration and iteration, and it's okay to refine or pivot your ideas based on feedback, market validation, or changing circumstances.

Understanding your interests is a foundational step in the entrepreneurial journey, guiding you towards business opportunities that align with your passions, values, and strengths. By gaining clarity on what truly motivates and excites you, you can embark on a path that not only leads to financial success but also fulfillment and satisfaction.

Chapter 3

Top Business Ideas for 2025

Low-Investment Businesses

The allure of being your own boss and building something from the ground up is undeniable. But for many, the fear of a hefty startup cost can be a major roadblock. Here's the good news: you don't need a mountain of cash to turn your entrepreneurial dreams into reality. In fact, 2025 presents a fertile ground for low-investment businesses to flourish. Here, we explore some of the most promising ideas, along with key considerations to set you on the path to success.

Capitalizing on the Digital Landscape:

The internet has revolutionized the business world, offering a plethora of opportunities that require minimal startup capital. Here are some exciting options:

- **Freelancing:** This is a classic low-investment business model. If you have a marketable skill, such as writing, graphic design, web development, or social media marketing, you can offer your services on freelance platforms like Upwork or Fiverr. The beauty lies in its flexibility – you can work part-time, full-time, or take on projects as they come.

- **E-commerce:** The e-commerce boom shows no signs of slowing down. With platforms like Shopify and Etsy making it easier than ever to set up an online store, you can sell anything from handcrafted goods to curated vintage finds.

- **Affiliate Marketing:** Here, you promote other companies' products or services and earn a commission on each sale you generate. This requires minimal upfront investment and leverages social media, content creation, or website traffic to attract potential customers.

- **Virtual Assistant Services:** Provide administrative, technical, or creative assistance to clients remotely. This is a rapidly growing field, and with good organizational skills and a willingness to learn, you can carve out a niche for yourself.

- **Online Coaching or Tutoring:** Share your expertise with a global audience by offering online courses or tutoring sessions. This could be anything from academic subjects to personal development or even fitness coaching. Platforms like Zoom and Teachable make conducting online sessions seamless.

Creative Fields and Service-Based Businesses:

☐ **Social Media Management:** Businesses increasingly recognize the power of social media but lack the time or expertise to manage it effectively. Here's where you step in. Offer social media management services, creating engaging content, managing accounts, and interacting with followers.

☐ **Content Creation:** Are you a skilled writer, videographer, or photographer? Businesses across industries crave high-quality content for their websites, social media, and marketing campaigns. This opens doors for freelance content creators, vloggers, and photographers.

☐ **Consulting:** If you have deep industry knowledge or expertise in a specific area, consider offering consulting services. This could involve business strategy, marketing advice, human resource management, or any niche where your experience holds value.

☐ **Home-based Services:** Offer services like pet sitting, house cleaning, or personal errands running. The low overhead costs make this a viable option, especially if you can leverage online platforms or local advertising to reach potential clients.

- ☐ **Event Planning:** If you thrive on meticulous organization and enjoy turning ideas into reality, event planning could be your forte. Start small with birthday parties or local gatherings, building a portfolio and client base before tackling larger events.

Emerging Trends and Niche Markets:

- ☐ **Subscription Boxes:** Curated subscription boxes catering to specific interests are gaining traction. This could involve beauty products, healthy snacks, crafting supplies, or anything with a dedicated following.

- ☐ **3D Printing Services:** 3D printing technology is becoming increasingly accessible. Offer 3D printing services, catering to designers, hobbyists, or businesses needing prototypes.

- ☐ **Online Fitness Coaching:** The fitness industry has gone virtual. Offer personalized online fitness coaching, creating customized workout plans and providing remote support to clients.

- **Pet Care Services:** The pet industry continues to boom. Explore specialized services like dog walking, pet grooming, or pet sitting, catering to busy pet owners.

Low-investment businesses present accessible opportunities for aspiring entrepreneurs to enter the market and pursue their entrepreneurial dreams with minimal financial risk. Whether it's online tutoring, freelance writing, virtual assistant services, or other digital ventures, there are countless opportunities for individuals to leverage their skills and expertise to create successful businesses in 2025 and beyond.

Tech-Driven Businesses

The year 2025 is a hotbed for technological innovation, and this presents a golden opportunity for entrepreneurs with a tech-savvy mind. While some tech ventures require significant capital investment, there's a wealth of exciting ideas that can be launched with minimal upfront costs. This guide explores some of the most promising tech-driven business ideas for 2025, along with practical tips to propel you towards success.

Leveraging Cutting-Edge Technologies:

The constant evolution of technology opens doors for innovative business models. Here are some ideas that harness the power of emerging tech:

- **Artificial Intelligence (AI) Applications:** AI is rapidly transforming industries. Consider developing AI-powered tools for specific sectors. This could involve AI-driven chatbots for customer service, AI-powered content creation for marketing agencies, or even AI-based diagnostics for healthcare providers.

- **Internet of Things (IoT) Solutions:** The interconnected world of the IoT offers immense potential. Develop smart home devices that automate daily tasks, create wearables that track health data, or design sensor-based solutions for industrial monitoring.

- **Blockchain-Based Services:** While cryptocurrencies garner much attention, blockchain technology has far-reaching implications. Explore building blockchain-based platforms for secure data storage, transparent supply chain management, or even innovative voting systems.

- **Augmented Reality (AR) and Virtual Reality (VR) Experiences:** The immersive worlds of AR and VR are gaining traction. Develop AR applications for education, training, or even product visualization. VR experiences could cater to the gaming industry, virtual tourism, or even architectural design.

- **Big Data Analytics Services:** The vast amounts of data generated daily hold immense value. Offer big data analytics services, helping businesses extract insights, optimize operations, and make data-driven decisions.

Building Businesses on Existing Platforms:

The tech giants have created powerful platforms that can serve as a springboard for your business. Here's how to leverage them:

- **Mobile App Development:** The mobile app market is saturated, but there's always room for innovative solutions. Develop a mobile app that addresses a specific need, offers a unique user experience, or caters to a niche market.

- **Software as a Service (SaaS) Solutions:** Create a cloud-based software application that solves a particular problem for businesses. This could be anything from project management tools to marketing automation software, all delivered on a subscription basis.

- **E-commerce Marketplaces:** Giant platforms like Amazon and Etsy provide fertile ground for e-commerce businesses.

Utilize these platforms to reach a wider audience, sell your products or services, and tap into established logistics networks.

☐ **On-Demand Service Platforms:** Platforms like Uber and DoorDash have revolutionized service delivery. Develop an on-demand service app catering to a specific need, such as dog walking, handyman services, or even on-demand laundry pickup and delivery.

☐ **Social Media Marketing and Advertising:** Social media platforms offer powerful marketing and advertising tools. Develop expertise in managing social media campaigns for businesses, creating engaging content, and driving targeted ad campaigns.

Catering to Specific Needs in the Tech Ecosystem:

Beyond developing your own tech solution, there are opportunities to serve the needs of the existing tech ecosystem:

☐ **Tech Support and Repair Services:** With the ever-increasing reliance on technology, demand for tech support and repair services remains high. Offer on-site or remote repair services for computers, mobile devices, or even smart home devices.

☐ **Cybersecurity Consulting:** Cybersecurity threats are a constant concern for businesses of all sizes. Offer cybersecurity consulting services, conducting vulnerability assessments, implementing security measures, and providing ongoing security training programs.

☐ **Data Migration and Cloud Storage Solutions:** As businesses migrate data to the cloud, data migration and cloud storage solutions are in high demand. Offer services to help businesses with secure data migration, cloud infrastructure setup, and ongoing cloud storage management.

☐ **E-learning and Online Training Solutions:** The tech industry is constantly evolving, requiring continuous learning. Develop e-learning courses or online training programs to equip individuals with the latest tech skills, cater to specific programming languages, or offer certification preparation courses.

☐ **Tech Talent Recruitment:** The tech industry has a constant need for skilled professionals. Specialize in tech talent recruitment, connecting qualified candidates with businesses across the tech sector

The tech revolution continues to reshape the business landscape, offering a plethora of opportunities for aspiring entrepreneurs. By leveraging your tech skills, identifying a niche market, and focusing on building a valuable solution, you can translate your idea into a thriving tech-driven business in 2025. Remember, success hinges on continuous learning, adaptation, and a commitment to providing exceptional value to your target audience. So, embrace the power of technology, unleash your creativity, and get ready to make your mark in the exciting world of tech entrepreneurship.

Sustainable & Socially Conscious Businesses

In the wake of global environmental challenges and increasing social awareness, sustainable and socially conscious businesses have gained significant traction in the entrepreneurial landscape of 2025. This section explores top business ideas that prioritize sustainability, ethical practices, and social impact, catering to consumers who seek environmentally friendly products, ethical business practices, and meaningful contributions to society.

1. Eco-Friendly Products:

With growing concerns about climate change and environmental degradation, there is a rising demand for eco-friendly products that minimize harm to the planet and promote sustainable living. Entrepreneurs can capitalize on this trend by launching businesses that offer a range of environmentally friendly alternatives to traditional products, spanning various industries and consumer needs.

From biodegradable packaging and reusable household goods to organic clothing and sustainable beauty products, there are countless opportunities for entrepreneurs to create eco-friendly alternatives that resonate with environmentally conscious consumers. By sourcing sustainable materials, minimizing waste, and adopting eco-friendly production processes, entrepreneurs can differentiate their products in the marketplace and appeal to a growing segment of environmentally conscious consumers.

Moreover, eco-friendly products can extend beyond consumer goods to encompass sustainable solutions for industries such as agriculture, construction, and transportation. Entrepreneurs can explore innovative technologies and business models that promote environmental sustainability and reduce carbon footprints across various sectors, contributing to a greener and more sustainable future.

2. Upcycling Services:

As the world grapples with mounting waste and limited resources, upcycling has emerged as a viable solution to reduce waste, conserve resources, and create value from discarded materials. Upcycling involves repurposing waste materials into new and useful products, offering entrepreneurs an opportunity to turn trash into treasure while promoting sustainability and creativity.

Entrepreneurs can launch upcycling businesses that specialize in repurposing specific materials, such as plastics, textiles, or electronic waste, into innovative and desirable products. Whether it's transforming old textiles into fashionable clothing, repurposing plastic bottles into household decor, or upcycling electronic components into new gadgets, the possibilities for upcycling are endless.

Moreover, upcycling businesses can also offer educational workshops, DIY kits, and consulting services to empower individuals and businesses to incorporate upcycling principles into their own practices. By raising awareness about the environmental benefits of upcycling and providing practical solutions for waste reduction, entrepreneurs can make a meaningful impact on sustainability and inspire others to adopt more eco-friendly lifestyles.

3. Local Food Delivery Ventures:

With growing concerns about food miles, carbon emissions, and the environmental impact of global supply chains, there is a growing demand for locally sourced and sustainably produced food products. Entrepreneurs can capitalize on this trend by launching local food delivery ventures that connect consumers with fresh, locally sourced produce and artisanal goods from nearby farms and producers.

Local food delivery ventures can take various forms, including subscription-based meal kits, farmers' market delivery services, or online marketplaces that connect consumers directly with local producers. By partnering with local farmers, artisans, and food producers, entrepreneurs can create a platform that promotes sustainable agriculture, supports local economies, and fosters community connections.

Moreover, local food delivery ventures can emphasize transparency, traceability, and ethical sourcing practices, providing consumers with information about the origins of their food and the farmers and producers behind it. By building trust and relationships with customers, entrepreneurs can differentiate their businesses in the competitive food delivery market and position themselves as champions of sustainability and social responsibility.

Sustainable and socially conscious businesses offer promising opportunities for entrepreneurs to make a positive impact on the planet and society while building successful and profitable ventures. Whether it's offering eco-friendly products, providing upcycling services, or launching local food delivery ventures, entrepreneurs can leverage their creativity, innovation, and commitment to sustainability to create businesses that align with their values and make a meaningful difference in the world. By prioritizing environmental stewardship, ethical practices, and social impact, entrepreneurs can build businesses that not only generate profits but also contribute to a more sustainable and equitable future for all.

Brick-and-Mortar Businesses

While digital technology has revolutionized many aspects of business, brick-and-mortar establishments continue to play a crucial role in local economies and communities worldwide. In this section, we explore top business ideas for 2025 that leverage the power of physical storefronts, personalized services, and community engagement to create unique and thriving brick-and-mortar businesses. From niche retail stores to personalized service businesses and local event catering, these ideas offer opportunities for entrepreneurs to establish a strong presence in their local markets and foster meaningful connections with customers.

1. Niche Retail Stores:

Despite the rise of e-commerce, there is still a demand for niche retail stores that offer specialized products, curated selections, and personalized shopping experiences. In 2025, entrepreneurs can capitalize on this demand by launching brick-and-mortar retail stores that cater to specific interests, hobbies, or lifestyle preferences, providing customers with unique offerings and memorable shopping experiences.

Examples of niche retail stores include specialty bookshops, vintage clothing boutiques, artisanal craft stores, and gourmet food shops. By focusing on a specific niche or target demographic, entrepreneurs can differentiate their stores from larger retailers and online competitors, attracting customers who seek unique and high-quality products that cannot be found elsewhere.

Moreover, niche retail stores can enhance the shopping experience through thoughtful merchandising, engaging displays, and personalized customer service. By creating a welcoming and immersive environment, entrepreneurs can cultivate loyal customer relationships, foster a sense of community, and establish their stores as destinations for enthusiasts and aficionados in their respective niches.

2. Personalized Service Businesses:

In an increasingly digital world, personalized services that cater to individual preferences, needs, and lifestyles are in high demand. Entrepreneurs can capitalize on this trend by launching brick-and-mortar businesses that offer personalized services in various industries, ranging from wellness and beauty to home services and professional development.

Examples of personalized service businesses include boutique fitness studios, beauty salons, pet grooming services, and career coaching centers. By providing customized experiences, tailored treatments, and one-on-one attention, entrepreneurs can create value for customers and differentiate their businesses in competitive markets.

Moreover, personalized service businesses can leverage technology to enhance the customer experience and streamline operations. Whether it's through online booking platforms, personalized recommendations, or customer relationship management systems, entrepreneurs can use technology to create seamless and efficient service delivery processes that delight customers and drive repeat business.

3. Local Event Catering:

In communities around the world, local events such as weddings, parties, and corporate gatherings are a significant source of business for caterers and event planners. Entrepreneurs can capitalize on this opportunity by launching brick-and-mortar businesses that specialize in providing catering services for local events, offering customized menus, and memorable dining experiences.

Local event catering businesses can cater to a variety of events, including weddings, birthdays, anniversaries, and corporate functions. By partnering with local venues, vendors, and event planners, entrepreneurs can establish their businesses as trusted partners in the local event industry, offering high-quality food and exceptional service that exceeds customer expectations.

Moreover, local event catering businesses can differentiate themselves by emphasizing sustainability, locally sourced ingredients, and creative culinary offerings. By aligning with the values and preferences of their target market, entrepreneurs can attract environmentally conscious customers and position their businesses as leaders in sustainable event catering.

Brick-and-mortar businesses continue to offer abundant opportunities for entrepreneurs to establish successful and thriving ventures in 2025. Whether it's niche retail stores, personalized service businesses, or local event catering, brick-and-mortar establishments play a vital role in local economies and communities, providing unique offerings, personalized experiences, and meaningful connections with customers. By embracing creativity, innovation, and a commitment to customer service, entrepreneurs can build brick-and-mortar businesses that stand out in competitive markets and contribute to the vibrancy and diversity of their local communities.

Chapter 4

Building Your Business

Crafting a Business Plan

Crafting a business plan is a foundational step in the journey of entrepreneurship. It serves as a roadmap for your business, guiding decision-making, setting goals, and charting a course for success. In this section, we explore the importance of crafting a comprehensive business plan and provide practical guidance on how to create one that aligns with your vision, objectives, and market realities.

Understanding the Purpose of a Business Plan:

Before diving into the specifics of crafting a business plan, it's essential to understand its purpose and significance in the entrepreneurial process. A business plan serves multiple functions, including:

- **Defining Your Vision and Mission:** A business plan helps you articulate your vision for the future of your business and clarify the purpose and values that drive your entrepreneurial endeavors.

☐ **Setting Goals and Objectives:** By establishing clear and measurable goals, a business plan provides a roadmap for achieving success and tracking progress over time.

☐ **Attracting Investors and Financing:** For startups and early-stage ventures, a well-crafted business plan is essential for attracting investors, securing financing, and convincing stakeholders of the viability and potential of your business concept.

☐ **Guiding Decision-Making:** A business plan serves as a reference point for making strategic decisions, allocating resources, and prioritizing initiatives to achieve business objectives.

☐ **Communicating with Stakeholders:** Whether it's employees, partners, or customers, a business plan communicates your vision, goals, and strategies to stakeholders and fosters alignment and collaboration.

Key Components of a Business Plan:

A comprehensive business plan typically includes the following key components:

- **Executive Summary:** A concise overview of your business concept, goals, and strategies, highlighting the most important aspects of your plan.

- **Company Description:** A detailed description of your business, including its mission, vision, values, legal structure, location, and history (if applicable).

- **Market Analysis:** An analysis of your target market, industry trends, competitive landscape, and customer demographics, providing insights into market opportunities and challenges.

- **Product or Service Offering:** A description of your products or services, including their features, benefits, unique selling propositions, and pricing strategies.

- **Marketing and Sales Strategy:** A plan for promoting and selling your products or services, including market positioning, branding, advertising, sales channels, and customer acquisition strategies.

- **Operational Plan:** An overview of your business operations, including production processes, supply chain management, inventory management, and facilities requirements.

- **Management and Organization:** Details about your management team, organizational structure, key personnel, and governance policies, highlighting their qualifications and roles in the business.

- **Financial Projections:** Forecasts of your business's financial performance, including income statements, cash flow projections, and balance sheets, based on assumptions about sales, expenses, and profitability.

- **Risk Assessment and Mitigation:** An analysis of potential risks and challenges facing your business, along with strategies for mitigating or managing them effectively.

- **Appendices:** Additional supporting documents, such as resumes of key personnel, market research reports, legal agreements, and other relevant materials.

Crafting Your Business Plan:

Crafting a business plan requires careful research, analysis, and strategic thinking. Here are some steps to help you create a comprehensive and effective business plan:

1. **Define Your Objectives:** Start by clarifying your business objectives, including short-term and long-term goals, and how you plan to measure success.

2. **Conduct Market Research:** Gather information about your target market, industry trends, competitor analysis, and customer preferences to inform your business strategy.

3. **Define Your Value Proposition:** Clearly articulate the value proposition of your products or services, including what sets them apart from competitors and why customers should choose your business.

4. **Develop Your Marketing and Sales Strategy:** Outline your marketing and sales tactics, including branding, advertising, promotions, pricing strategies, and distribution channels.

5. **Create Financial Projections:** Develop realistic financial projections based on your sales forecasts, expense estimates, pricing models, and funding requirements.

6. **Address Operational Considerations:** Consider the operational aspects of your business, including production processes, supply chain management, logistics, and facilities requirements.

7. **Outline Your Management and Organizational Structure:** Define the roles and responsibilities of key personnel, including yourself, and outline the organizational structure of your business.

8. **Assess Risks and Contingency Plans:** Identify potential risks and challenges facing your business and develop strategies for mitigating or managing them effectively.

9. **Review and Revise:** Once you've drafted your business plan, review it carefully, seeking feedback from mentors, advisors, or industry experts, and revise as needed to ensure clarity, accuracy, and feasibility.

Crafting a business plan is a critical step in the process of building a successful business. By defining your vision, setting clear goals, and developing a strategic roadmap, you can navigate the complexities of entrepreneurship with confidence and clarity. Whether you're seeking financing, attracting investors, or simply guiding your own decision-making, a well-crafted business plan serves as a valuable tool for achieving your entrepreneurial aspirations and realizing your business's full potential.

Finding Your Audience & Building a Brand

In the competitive landscape of entrepreneurship, finding your audience and building a strong brand are essential components of building a successful business. This section explores the importance of understanding your target audience, defining your brand identity, and developing strategies to engage and connect with customers effectively.

Understanding Your Target Audience:

One of the fundamental steps in building a successful business is understanding your target audience—the individuals or groups of people who are most likely to buy your products or services. By gaining insight into their demographics, preferences, needs, and behaviors, you can tailor your offerings, messaging, and marketing strategies to resonate with your target audience effectively.

Market research plays a crucial role in understanding your target audience. This can involve quantitative methods such as surveys and data analysis, as well as qualitative approaches like interviews, focus groups, and observation. By gathering information about your target audience's demographics, psychographics, purchasing habits, and pain points, you can develop a deeper understanding of who they are and what they need.

Segmentation is another important aspect of identifying your target audience. Rather than trying to appeal to everyone, segment your audience into distinct groups based on shared characteristics or needs. This allows you to tailor your marketing efforts to specific segments, providing more relevant and personalized messaging that resonates with their interests and preferences.

Defining Your Brand Identity:

Once you've identified your target audience, the next step is to define your brand identity—the unique personality, values, and characteristics that set your business apart from competitors and resonate with customers. Your brand identity encompasses elements such as your brand name, logo, colors, typography, voice, and messaging, as well as your mission, vision, and values.

Developing a strong brand identity starts with defining your brand's purpose and values—the underlying principles and beliefs that guide your business decisions and actions. What do you stand for? What do you want to be known for? By articulating your brand's purpose and values, you can create a clear and compelling brand story that resonates with your target audience and builds emotional connections.

Visual branding elements, such as your logo, colors, and typography, play a crucial role in shaping your brand identity and conveying your brand's personality and aesthetic. Choose visual elements that reflect your brand's values, evoke the desired emotions, and resonate with your target audience. Consistency is key—ensure that your visual branding is cohesive across all touchpoints, including your website, social media profiles, marketing materials, and physical storefronts.

In addition to visual branding, your brand voice and messaging are also essential components of your brand identity. Your brand voice—the tone, style, and language used in your communications—should be consistent and reflective of your brand's personality and values. Whether it's casual and friendly, professional and authoritative, or playful and creative, your brand voice should resonate with your target audience and reinforce your brand identity.

Building Your Brand:

Building a strong brand requires a multi-faceted approach that encompasses both online and offline strategies. Here are some key strategies for building your brand effectively:

1. **Create Compelling Content:** Develop high-quality, relevant content that educates, entertains, and engages your target audience. This can include blog posts, videos, podcasts, social media posts, and email newsletters that provide value to your audience and showcase your expertise.

2. **Engage on Social Media:** Build a presence on social media platforms where your target audience spends time, and engage with them regularly through posts, comments, messages, and interactions. Share content that resonates with your audience, encourages engagement, and fosters community building.

3. **Offer Exceptional Customer Service:** Provide outstanding customer service that exceeds customer expectations and reinforces your brand's commitment to excellence. Respond promptly to inquiries, address concerns and complaints professionally, and go above and beyond to delight your customers at every touchpoint.

4. **Build Relationships with Influencers:** Collaborate with influencers and thought leaders in your industry who

have a following that aligns with your target audience. Partner with influencers to promote your brand, share your content, and endorse your products or services, leveraging their credibility and reach to expand your brand's visibility and credibility.

5. **Participate in Community Events:** Get involved in local events, festivals, trade shows, and community gatherings where you can showcase your brand, interact with customers face-to-face, and build relationships with members of your community. Sponsorship, booths, and speaking engagements are excellent opportunities to raise brand awareness and connect with potential customers.

6. **Collect and Act on Feedback:** Solicit feedback from your customers through surveys, reviews, and testimonials, and use this feedback to improve your products, services, and customer experience continually. Show customers that their opinions matter and that you are committed to delivering value and meeting their needs.

7. **Measure and Monitor Your Brand Performance:** Use analytics tools and metrics to track the performance of your branding efforts, including website traffic, social media engagement, customer satisfaction scores, and brand sentiment. Monitor trends over time, identify

areas for improvement, and adjust your strategies accordingly to ensure that your brand continues to resonate with your target audience and drive business results.

Finding your audience and building a strong brand are essential components of building a successful business. By understanding your target audience, defining your brand identity, and developing strategies to engage and connect with customers effectively, you can differentiate your business in a competitive marketplace, foster customer loyalty, and drive long-term success. Whether you're a startup or an established business, investing in your brand's identity and reputation is a strategic imperative that can set you apart from competitors and position you for growth and profitability in the years to come.

Leveraging Technology & Online Tools

Technology and online tools have become indispensable assets for businesses of all sizes. From streamlining operations to expanding reach and enhancing customer experiences, leveraging technology effectively can significantly impact the success and growth of your business. This section explores the myriad ways in which entrepreneurs can harness the power of technology and online tools to build and scale their businesses efficiently and effectively.

The Role of Technology in Business:

Technology has transformed the way businesses operate, enabling them to automate processes, streamline workflows, and access valuable insights to make informed decisions. By leveraging technology effectively, businesses can gain a competitive edge, improve efficiency, and drive innovation across all aspects of their operations.

One of the primary benefits of technology in business is its ability to increase productivity. Through the automation of repetitive tasks, the implementation of project management software, and the use of communication tools, businesses can streamline workflows and free up time for employees to focus on high-value activities.

Technology also plays a crucial role in enhancing collaboration and communication within organizations. With the rise of remote work and distributed teams, tools such as video conferencing, instant messaging, and collaboration platforms enable employees to connect and collaborate seamlessly, regardless of their location.

Furthermore, technology empowers businesses to gather and analyze data to gain valuable insights into customer behavior, market trends, and business performance. By leveraging analytics tools and data-driven decision-making, businesses can identify opportunities for growth, optimize processes, and improve the customer experience.

Online Tools for Business Success:

The proliferation of online tools and software solutions has democratized access to powerful resources that were once only available to large enterprises. Whether it's project management, marketing, sales, or customer relationship management, there is a plethora of online tools available to help businesses streamline operations, automate tasks, and drive growth.

- **Project Management:** Project management tools such as Asana, Trello, and Basecamp help businesses organize tasks, track progress, and collaborate effectively on projects. These tools enable teams to set goals, assign responsibilities, and monitor deadlines to ensure projects are completed on time and within budget.

- **Marketing Automation:** Marketing automation platforms like HubSpot, Marketo, and Mailchimp enable businesses to automate marketing processes, such as email campaigns, social media scheduling, and lead nurturing. By automating repetitive tasks and workflows, businesses can save time and resources while delivering personalized and targeted marketing messages to their audience.

- **Customer Relationship Management (CRM):** CRM software such as Salesforce, Zoho CRM, and HubSpot CRM help businesses manage customer interactions, track leads, and nurture relationships throughout the customer lifecycle. By centralizing customer data and providing insights into customer behavior, CRM systems empower businesses to deliver personalized experiences and drive customer loyalty.

- **E-commerce Platforms:** E-commerce platforms like Shopify, WooCommerce, and Magento provide businesses with the tools they need to build and manage online stores effectively. These platforms offer features such as inventory management, payment processing, and customizable storefronts, enabling businesses to create seamless and secure online shopping experiences for their customers.

- **Analytics and Reporting:** Analytics tools such as Google Analytics, Adobe Analytics, and Mixpanel enable businesses to track website traffic, user engagement, and conversion rates to gain insights into their online performance. By analyzing data and generating reports, businesses can identify areas for improvement, optimize marketing strategies, and measure the impact of their efforts.

☐ **Customer Support and Communication:** Customer support tools like Zendesk, Freshdesk, and Intercom help businesses provide exceptional customer service through various channels, including email, live chat, and social media. These tools enable businesses to manage customer inquiries efficiently, resolve issues promptly, and deliver personalized support experiences.

Integrating Technology into Your Business Strategy:

To leverage technology effectively, businesses must integrate it into their overall business strategy and culture. Here are some key considerations for integrating technology into your business strategy:

1. **Align Technology with Business Goals:** Start by identifying your business goals and objectives, and then determine how technology can support and enhance these goals. Whether it's improving efficiency, increasing

sales, or enhancing the customer experience, technology should align with your broader business strategy.

2. **Invest in Training and Education:** Provide training and education for employees to ensure they have the skills and knowledge needed to effectively leverage technology in their roles. This may involve offering workshops, online courses, or one-on-one coaching to help employees understand how to use technology tools and platforms efficiently.

3. **Stay Agile and Flexible:** In today's rapidly changing business landscape, it's essential to stay agile and flexible in your approach to technology. Be open to experimenting with new tools and technologies, and be willing to adapt and iterate based on feedback and changing market conditions.

4. **Focus on Data Security:** With the increasing prevalence of cyber threats and data breaches, data security should be a top priority for businesses. Implement robust security measures, such as encryption, multi-factor authentication, and regular security audits, to protect sensitive data and mitigate risks.

5. **Monitor Performance and ROI:** Continuously monitor the performance of your technology investments and assess their return on investment (ROI). Track key

metrics, such as productivity gains, cost savings, and revenue growth, to evaluate the impact of technology on your business and make informed decisions about future investments.

Leveraging technology and online tools is essential for building and scaling a successful business in today's digital age. By harnessing the power of technology to streamline operations, enhance communication, and drive growth, businesses can gain a competitive edge, improve efficiency, and deliver exceptional experiences to their customers. Whether it's project management, marketing automation, customer relationship management, or e-commerce platforms, there are countless online tools available to help businesses achieve their goals and succeed in today's dynamic business landscape. By integrating technology into their overall business strategy and culture, businesses can position themselves for long-term success and thrive in an increasingly digital world.

Building a Strong Online Presence

Having a strong online presence is essential for businesses of all sizes. Whether you're a startup or an established brand, the internet offers unparalleled opportunities to connect with customers, expand your reach, and build a loyal following. This section explores the importance of building a strong online presence and provides practical strategies for businesses to establish and enhance their digital footprint effectively.

The Importance of an Online Presence:

In today's interconnected world, consumers increasingly turn to the internet to discover, research, and engage with businesses. Whether they're searching for products, services, or information, having a strong online presence ensures that your business is visible, accessible, and relevant to your target audience. Here are some key reasons why building a strong online presence is crucial for business success:

- **Reach and Visibility:** With billions of people using the internet every day, having an online presence allows businesses to reach a global audience and increase their visibility exponentially. By establishing a presence on search engines, social media platforms, and other online channels, businesses can attract potential customers from around the world and expand their reach far beyond their local market.

- **Credibility and Trust:** A well-designed website, active social media profiles, and positive online reviews can enhance a business's credibility and build trust with customers. An online presence provides a platform for businesses to showcase their expertise, share customer testimonials, and demonstrate their commitment to quality, reliability, and customer satisfaction.

☐ **Customer Engagement and Interaction:** Through social media, email marketing, and other online channels, businesses can engage with customers in real-time, respond to inquiries, address concerns, and provide personalized support. By fostering two-way communication and building relationships with customers, businesses can create meaningful connections that drive loyalty and repeat business.

☐ **Competitive Advantage:** In today's competitive marketplace, having a strong online presence can give businesses a significant advantage over competitors. By staying ahead of trends, embracing new technologies, and delivering exceptional online experiences, businesses can differentiate themselves and stand out in crowded markets.

Strategies for Building a Strong Online Presence:

Building a strong online presence requires a strategic and multi-faceted approach that encompasses various digital channels and tactics. Here are some key strategies for businesses to establish and enhance their online presence effectively:

1. **Create a Professional Website:** Your website serves as the digital storefront for your business and is often the first impression customers have of your brand. Invest in creating a professional, user-friendly website that reflects your brand identity, showcases your products or services, and provides valuable content and resources for visitors.

2. **Optimize for Search Engines:** Search engine optimization (SEO) is essential for improving your website's visibility and ranking in search engine results pages (SERPs). Conduct keyword research, optimize your website's meta tags, headers, and content, and build high-quality backlinks to improve your site's SEO and attract organic traffic.

3. **Utilize Social Media:** Social media platforms such as Facebook, Instagram, Twitter, LinkedIn, and YouTube offer powerful opportunities for businesses to engage with customers, share content, and build brand awareness. Choose the platforms that are most relevant to your target audience and develop a consistent presence by posting regularly, interacting with followers, and sharing valuable content.

4. **Create Valuable Content:** Content marketing is a cornerstone of building a strong online presence. Create high-quality, relevant content that educates, entertains, and engages your target audience. This can include blog posts, articles, videos, infographics, podcasts, and social media posts that address customer pain points, answer common questions, and provide value.

5. **Engage in Email Marketing:** Email marketing remains one of the most effective channels for nurturing leads, driving conversions, and building relationships with customers. Build an email list of subscribers interested in your products or services, and send targeted, personalized emails that deliver value and encourage action.

6. **Invest in Paid Advertising:** Paid advertising, such as pay-per-click (PPC) ads, display ads, and social media ads, can help businesses increase visibility, drive traffic, and generate leads quickly. Develop targeted ad campaigns that align with your business goals and target audience, and monitor and optimize your campaigns for maximum effectiveness.

7. **Monitor and Manage Online Reviews:** Online reviews and ratings have a significant impact on a business's reputation and credibility. Encourage satisfied customers to leave positive reviews on platforms like Google My

Business, Yelp, and Facebook, and promptly respond to negative reviews to address concerns and demonstrate your commitment to customer satisfaction.

8. **Track and Analyze Performance:** Use analytics tools and metrics to track the performance of your online presence, including website traffic, social media engagement, email open rates, and conversion rates. Analyze data regularly to identify trends, opportunities, and areas for improvement, and adjust your strategies accordingly to optimize your online presence.

Building a strong online presence is essential for businesses to succeed and thrive in today's digital world. By establishing a professional website, optimizing for search engines, leveraging social media, creating valuable content, engaging in email marketing, investing in paid advertising, managing online reviews, and tracking performance, businesses can build a robust and impactful online presence that attracts customers, builds trust, and drives growth. Whether you're a small startup or a large corporation, investing in your online presence is a strategic imperative that can set you apart from competitors, foster customer loyalty, and position your business for long-term success in the digital age.

Chapter 5

The Future of Work

Adapting to Future Trends

The future of work is a topic of increasing significance as businesses navigate a rapidly changing landscape shaped by technological advancements, demographic shifts, and evolving consumer preferences. In this section, we explore key future trends impacting the world of work and discuss strategies for businesses to adapt and thrive in the face of these transformative changes.

1. Rise of Remote Work:

The COVID-19 pandemic accelerated the adoption of remote work, prompting businesses worldwide to embrace flexible work arrangements and remote collaboration tools. As we look to the future, remote work is expected to remain a prominent feature of the work landscape, driven by advances in technology, changing employee expectations, and the growing acceptance of remote work as a viable alternative to traditional office-based environments.

For businesses, adapting to the rise of remote work involves investing in technology infrastructure, implementing remote work policies and procedures, and fostering a culture of trust, accountability, and collaboration among remote teams. By providing employees with the tools, resources, and support they need to succeed in a remote work environment, businesses can harness the benefits of remote work, such as increased productivity, flexibility, and talent retention, while mitigating the challenges associated with remote collaboration and communication.

2. Embrace of Digital Transformation:

Digital transformation has become a strategic imperative for businesses seeking to remain competitive and resilient in an increasingly digital world. From cloud computing and artificial intelligence to data analytics and automation, businesses are leveraging technology to streamline operations, enhance customer experiences, and drive innovation across all aspects of their operations.

To adapt to the embrace of digital transformation, businesses must prioritize investment in digital capabilities, talent, and infrastructure. This includes adopting agile methodologies, fostering a culture of experimentation and learning, and empowering employees to embrace digital tools and technologies in their roles. By embracing digital transformation, businesses can unlock new opportunities for growth, efficiency, and innovation, while staying ahead of competitors and meeting the evolving needs of customers in the digital age.

3. Focus on Sustainability and Social Responsibility:

As concerns about climate change, environmental degradation, and social inequality continue to rise, businesses are facing increasing pressure to prioritize sustainability and social responsibility in their operations. Consumers are increasingly seeking out brands that demonstrate a commitment to environmental stewardship, social justice, and ethical business practices, influencing purchasing decisions and brand loyalty.

To adapt to this trend, businesses must integrate sustainability and social responsibility into their business strategies, operations, and corporate culture. This includes reducing carbon emissions, minimizing waste, sourcing ethically and sustainably, and supporting social initiatives that benefit employees, communities, and society at large. By aligning with the values and preferences of customers and stakeholders, businesses can enhance their reputation, build trust, and create long-term value for all stakeholders.

4. Emphasis on Agility and Resilience:

In today's volatile and uncertain business environment, agility and resilience have become essential attributes for businesses seeking to navigate disruption, uncertainty, and rapid change. Whether it's economic volatility, technological disruption, or global pandemics, businesses must be prepared to adapt quickly and effectively to emerging challenges and opportunities.

To adapt to the emphasis on agility and resilience, businesses must cultivate a mindset of adaptability, flexibility, and innovation throughout the organization. This includes empowering employees to take initiative, experiment, and learn from failure, as well as fostering cross-functional collaboration, knowledge sharing, and continuous improvement. By building organizational resilience and agility, businesses can respond more effectively to change, capitalize on emerging opportunities, and thrive in an increasingly complex and unpredictable business landscape.

As we look to the future of work, businesses must embrace change, innovation, and adaptability to succeed in an increasingly dynamic and interconnected world. By embracing remote work, digital transformation, sustainability, and resilience, businesses can position themselves for long-term success and create value for all stakeholders. The future of work holds both challenges and opportunities, and businesses that are proactive, agile, and forward-thinking will be best positioned to thrive in the years ahead.

Embracing Change: Opportunities in Disruption

In the ever-evolving landscape of work, disruption has become the new norm. From technological advancements to global crises, businesses are continually facing challenges that require them to adapt, innovate, and evolve. In this section, we explore the concept of embracing change as an opportunity for growth and transformation in the future of work.

1. Embracing Technological Advancements:

Technological advancements, such as artificial intelligence, automation, and the Internet of Things, are reshaping industries and transforming the way we work. While these advancements may disrupt traditional business models and workflows, they also present opportunities for businesses to innovate, improve efficiency, and create new value for customers.

For businesses, embracing technological advancements involves staying informed about emerging technologies, investing in digital capabilities, and fostering a culture of innovation and experimentation. By embracing automation, businesses can streamline repetitive tasks, increase productivity, and free up employees to focus on higher-value activities. Similarly, by leveraging artificial intelligence and data analytics, businesses can gain valuable insights, personalize customer experiences, and make data-driven decisions that drive business growth.

2. Adapting to Remote Work:

The rise of remote work has fundamentally transformed the way businesses operate, challenging traditional notions of office-based work and collaboration. While remote work presents unique challenges, such as communication barriers and work-life balance issues, it also offers opportunities for businesses to tap into a global talent pool, reduce overhead costs, and promote flexibility and autonomy among employees.

To adapt to remote work, businesses must invest in remote collaboration tools, establish clear communication channels, and provide training and support for remote employees. By embracing remote work, businesses can access a diverse talent pool, foster a culture of trust and empowerment, and create more flexible and resilient organizations capable of adapting to changing market conditions and workforce preferences.

3. Seizing Opportunities in Crisis:

While crises, such as pandemics, economic downturns, and natural disasters, can pose significant challenges for businesses, they also present opportunities for innovation, adaptation, and growth. During times of crisis, businesses that are agile, resilient, and forward-thinking can seize opportunities to pivot their business models, expand into new markets, and address emerging customer needs.

For businesses, seizing opportunities in crisis involves staying agile and responsive to changing market dynamics, identifying emerging trends and opportunities, and taking calculated risks to capitalize on them. By embracing uncertainty and disruption as opportunities for growth and transformation, businesses can emerge stronger, more resilient, and better positioned for success in the future.

4. Fostering a Culture of Adaptability:

In a rapidly changing business environment, fostering a culture of adaptability is essential for businesses to thrive and succeed. A culture of adaptability encourages employees to embrace change, challenge the status quo, and continuously seek out new opportunities for improvement and innovation.

To foster a culture of adaptability, businesses must lead by example, empower employees to take ownership of their work, and encourage open communication and collaboration across all levels of the organization. By creating an environment where experimentation, creativity, and learning are valued and rewarded, businesses can cultivate a workforce that is resilient, agile, and capable of navigating uncertainty and disruption with confidence and resilience.

The future of work is characterized by constant change, disruption, and uncertainty. However, within this disruption lies opportunities for businesses to innovate, adapt, and thrive. By embracing technological advancements, adapting to remote work, seizing opportunities in crisis, and fostering a culture of adaptability, businesses can position themselves for success in the future of work. The key lies in embracing change as an opportunity for growth and transformation, rather than a threat to be feared. By embracing change, businesses can unlock new opportunities, drive innovation, and create value for customers, employees, and stakeholders alike.

Chapter 6

Real-life Examples of Successful Businesses

Low-Investment Businesses

In the realm of entrepreneurship, the notion that significant capital is required to start a successful business is being challenged by a growing number of low-investment business ventures. These ventures demonstrate that with innovation, creativity, and strategic thinking, entrepreneurs can launch and grow profitable businesses without the need for substantial financial resources. In this section, we explore real-life examples of low-investment businesses that have achieved remarkable success, offering inspiration and insights for aspiring entrepreneurs.

1. Online Tutoring Platforms:

Online tutoring platforms have emerged as a lucrative business opportunity, providing students with access to personalized learning experiences while offering tutors a flexible and scalable way to monetize their expertise. Companies like Khan Academy, Chegg Tutors, and Tutor.com have revolutionized the education industry by connecting students with qualified tutors through online platforms, offering a wide range of subjects and topics at affordable rates.

These platforms typically require minimal upfront investment, as they leverage existing technology infrastructure and rely on freelance tutors to deliver their services. By charging a commission or subscription fee for access to their platform, online tutoring companies can generate revenue while providing value to both students and tutors. With the increasing demand for remote learning solutions and the growing popularity of online education, the online tutoring industry is poised for continued growth and innovation in the years to come.

2. Freelance Writing Services:

The rise of the gig economy has created abundant opportunities for freelance writers to build successful businesses offering content creation services to clients worldwide. Freelance writers can leverage their writing skills and expertise to provide a wide range of content, including articles, blog posts, web copy, and marketing materials, to businesses, publications, and individuals in need of high-quality written content.

Freelance writers typically require minimal investment to get started, as they can work from home using basic tools such as a computer and internet connection. By building a portfolio of work, establishing a strong online presence, and networking with potential clients, freelance writers can attract clients and command competitive rates for their services. With the increasing demand for content in today's digital world, freelance writing presents a low-investment business opportunity with significant potential for growth and success.

3. Virtual Assistant Services:

Virtual assistant services have become increasingly popular among businesses and entrepreneurs seeking administrative support without the overhead costs of hiring full-time employees. Virtual assistants provide a wide range of services, including email management, scheduling, research, social media management, and customer support, allowing clients to focus on their core business activities while delegating time-consuming tasks to skilled professionals.

Starting a virtual assistant business typically requires minimal investment, as virtual assistants can work remotely using common tools such as email, calendar apps, project management software, and communication platforms. By marketing their services online, networking with potential clients, and delivering exceptional results, virtual assistants can build a profitable business with low overhead costs and high demand for their services. With the rise of remote work and the increasing need for flexible administrative support, the virtual assistant industry is poised for continued growth and expansion in the years ahead.

4. Dropshipping E-commerce Stores:

Dropshipping has emerged as a popular business model for entrepreneurs looking to start an e-commerce business with minimal upfront investment. In a dropshipping business, entrepreneurs partner with suppliers who handle inventory management, storage, and shipping, allowing them to focus on marketing, sales, and customer service. By creating an online store, sourcing products from suppliers, and driving traffic to their website, dropshippers can generate revenue without the need for inventory or warehouse space.

Dropshipping e-commerce stores require minimal investment to get started, as entrepreneurs can use e-commerce platforms like Shopify or WooCommerce to set up their online store and source products from suppliers without purchasing inventory upfront. By focusing on niche markets, identifying trending products, and optimizing their marketing and sales processes, dropshippers can build a profitable e-commerce business with low overhead costs and the potential for scalability and growth.

Low-investment businesses offer aspiring entrepreneurs an accessible and affordable path to entrepreneurship, allowing them to launch and grow successful businesses without the need for substantial financial resources. From online tutoring platforms and freelance writing services to virtual assistant agencies and dropshipping e-commerce stores, these real-life examples demonstrate the diversity and potential of low-investment business ventures. By leveraging their skills, creativity, and strategic thinking, entrepreneurs can capitalize on emerging opportunities and build thriving businesses that generate income and create value for customers and stakeholders alike.

Tech-Driven Businesses

Tech-driven businesses leverage cutting-edge technologies to disrupt industries, solve complex problems, and deliver innovative products and services to customers. In this section, we explore real-life examples of tech-driven businesses that have achieved remarkable success by harnessing the power of technology to transform industries and create value in new and exciting ways.

1. Airbnb:

Founded in 2008 by Brian Chesky, Joe Gebbia, and Nathan Blecharczyk, Airbnb has revolutionized the hospitality industry by providing a platform for people to rent out their homes, apartments, and other accommodations to travelers. Through its innovative online marketplace, Airbnb connects hosts with guests looking for unique and authentic travel experiences, offering a wide range of lodging options at various price points and locations around the world.

At the heart of Airbnb's success is its use of technology to facilitate seamless transactions, streamline the booking process, and enhance the user experience for both hosts and guests. The platform employs advanced algorithms and machine learning algorithms to match guests with suitable accommodations based on their preferences, search history, and other factors. By leveraging technology, Airbnb has transformed the way people travel, enabling them to discover new destinations, connect with local hosts, and experience destinations like a local.

2. Uber:

Uber, founded in 2009 by Travis Kalanick and Garrett Camp, has disrupted the transportation industry by providing an innovative ride-hailing service that connects passengers with drivers through a mobile app. By leveraging GPS technology, real-time data analytics, and seamless payment processing, Uber has transformed the way people commute, offering a convenient, affordable, and efficient alternative to traditional taxis and public transportation.

Uber's success lies in its ability to harness technology to optimize routes, match drivers with passengers, and provide a seamless end-to-end transportation experience. The company's sophisticated algorithms analyze traffic patterns, demand forecasts, and driver availability to ensure efficient service and minimize wait times for passengers. By embracing technology and data-driven decision-making, Uber has become a global leader in the ride-hailing industry, disrupting traditional transportation models and revolutionizing urban mobility.

3. SpaceX:

SpaceX, founded in 2002 by Elon Musk, is revolutionizing the aerospace industry through its ambitious mission to make space exploration more accessible and affordable. By developing advanced rocket technology, reusable launch vehicles, and innovative spacecraft designs, SpaceX is paving the way for human colonization of Mars and enabling new opportunities for scientific research, satellite deployment, and commercial space travel.

At the core of SpaceX's success is its relentless focus on innovation, engineering excellence, and cost-effective space launch solutions. The company's Falcon rockets and Dragon spacecraft leverage cutting-edge technologies, such as advanced propulsion systems, autonomous landing capabilities, and 3D printing, to reduce the cost of space travel and increase the reliability of space missions. By pushing the boundaries of space exploration and challenging traditional aerospace models, SpaceX is driving innovation and inspiring the next generation of space explorers.

4. Zoom:

Zoom, founded in 2011 by Eric Yuan, has become a household name in the video conferencing industry, providing a user-friendly platform for virtual meetings, webinars, and remote collaboration. With its intuitive interface, high-quality audio and video, and robust features such as screen sharing and chat, Zoom has transformed the way people communicate and collaborate in both professional and personal settings.

Zoom's success lies in its ability to leverage cloud computing, scalable infrastructure, and adaptive streaming technology to deliver a reliable and secure video conferencing experience. The platform's ease of use, cross-platform compatibility, and affordability have made it a popular choice for businesses, educational institutions, and individuals around the world, particularly during the COVID-19 pandemic when remote work and virtual communication became essential.

Tech-driven businesses are at the forefront of innovation, driving transformation across industries and creating new opportunities for growth and success. From disruptive startups like Airbnb and Uber to visionary companies like SpaceX and Zoom, these real-life examples demonstrate the power of technology to revolutionize markets, disrupt traditional business models, and create value for customers and stakeholders. By embracing technology, fostering a culture of innovation, and leveraging data-driven insights, tech-driven businesses can thrive in today's fast-paced and ever-changing business landscape, shaping the future of industries and driving economic growth and prosperity.

Sustainable & Socially Conscious Businesses

In recent years, there has been a growing recognition of the importance of sustainability and social responsibility in business. Sustainable and socially conscious businesses prioritize environmental stewardship, social impact, and ethical business practices, demonstrating a commitment to creating value for both society and the planet. In this section, we explore real-life examples of successful businesses that have integrated sustainability and social responsibility into their core values and business models, inspiring positive change and making a difference in the world.

1. Patagonia:

Patagonia, founded in 1973 by Yvon Chouinard, is a leading outdoor apparel company renowned for its commitment to environmental sustainability and corporate social responsibility. From its inception, Patagonia has placed a strong emphasis on minimizing its environmental footprint, sourcing sustainable materials, and advocating for environmental conservation and activism.

Patagonia's success lies in its holistic approach to sustainability, which encompasses every aspect of its business operations, from design and manufacturing to distribution and retail. The company invests in innovative materials and production methods to reduce waste, minimize water and energy consumption, and lower its carbon footprint. Patagonia also advocates for environmental causes and supports grassroots organizations working to protect the planet's natural resources.

Through initiatives such as "1% for the Planet," Patagonia donates a portion of its sales revenue to environmental organizations, contributing millions of dollars to conservation efforts worldwide. By aligning its business practices with its values and principles, Patagonia has earned the trust and loyalty of customers who share its commitment to sustainability and social responsibility.

2. TOMS:

TOMS, founded in 2006 by Blake Mycoskie, is a footwear company known for its innovative "One for One" business model, which pledges to donate a pair of shoes to a child in need for every pair of shoes purchased. Inspired by a trip to Argentina, where Mycoskie witnessed the impact of children living without shoes, TOMS was founded on the belief that businesses can be a force for good in the world.

Since its inception, TOMS has expanded its mission to include eyewear, clean water, and safe birth initiatives, providing eyeglasses, clean water, and maternal healthcare services to people in need around the world. Through its philanthropic efforts and commitment to social impact, TOMS has become a leading example of a socially conscious business that prioritizes giving back to communities and making a positive difference in people's lives.

TOMS' success is rooted in its ability to engage customers in its mission and values, creating a sense of purpose and meaning beyond the products it sells. By aligning its business objectives with its social mission, TOMS has built a loyal customer base and cultivated a strong brand identity centered around compassion, empathy, and social responsibility.

3. Seventh Generation:

Seventh Generation, founded in 1988 by Jeffrey Hollender, is a household and personal care products company committed to producing environmentally friendly, non-toxic products that are safe for people and the planet. With a focus on transparency, sustainability, and corporate accountability, Seventh Generation has become a pioneer in the green cleaning and household products industry.

Seventh Generation's product line includes a wide range of household cleaners, laundry detergents, diapers, and personal care items made from plant-based ingredients and renewable materials. The company is dedicated to reducing its environmental impact through initiatives such as carbon neutrality, waste reduction, and sustainable sourcing practices.

Seventh Generation's commitment to sustainability extends beyond its products to its business practices and operations. The company invests in renewable energy, offsets its carbon emissions, and advocates for policies that promote environmental conservation and public health. By prioritizing sustainability and transparency, Seventh Generation has earned the trust and loyalty of consumers who value eco-friendly products and ethical business practices.

4. Beyond Meat:

Beyond Meat, founded in 2009 by Ethan Brown, is a plant-based meat substitute company that is revolutionizing the food industry with its innovative approach to sustainable and ethical food production. By creating delicious, nutrient-rich plant-based alternatives to traditional meat products, Beyond Meat is addressing the environmental and ethical concerns associated with conventional animal agriculture.

Beyond Meat's products, which include plant-based burgers, sausages, and meatballs, are made from ingredients such as peas, beans, and other plant-based proteins, offering a healthier, more sustainable alternative to animal-based meat products. The company's products are free from antibiotics, hormones, and GMOs, making them a popular choice among consumers seeking healthier and more environmentally friendly food options.

Beyond Meat's success lies in its ability to replicate the taste, texture, and mouthfeel of traditional meat products using plant-based ingredients and innovative food technology. By partnering with restaurants, fast-food chains, and grocery stores to offer its products to a wider audience, Beyond Meat is making plant-based eating more accessible and appealing to consumers around the world. Through its commitment to sustainability, animal welfare, and public health, Beyond Meat is leading the way toward a more sustainable and ethical food system.

Sustainable and socially conscious businesses are demonstrating that profitability and social impact are not mutually exclusive. By integrating sustainability, environmental stewardship, and social responsibility into their business models and operations, companies like Patagonia, TOMS, Seventh Generation, and Beyond Meat are proving that businesses can be a force for positive change in the world. Through their innovative products, ethical practices, and commitment to making a difference, these businesses are inspiring others to follow suit and create a more sustainable and socially responsible future for generations to come.

Brick-and-Mortar Businesses

In an era dominated by e-commerce and digital innovation, brick-and-mortar businesses continue to play a vital role in local economies and communities worldwide. While online shopping offers convenience and accessibility, brick-and-mortar stores provide unique experiences, personalized service, and a tangible connection to products and brands. In this section, we explore real-life examples of successful brick-and-mortar businesses that have thrived by embracing innovation, customer-centricity, and community engagement.

1. Apple:

Apple, founded by Steve Jobs, Steve Wozniak, and Ronald Wayne in 1976, has become synonymous with innovation, design excellence, and customer experience in the technology industry. While Apple is best known for its iconic products like the iPhone, iPad, and Mac, the company's retail stores have also played a crucial role in its success. With over 500 stores worldwide, Apple's retail stores are designed to provide customers with immersive experiences, personalized service, and hands-on demonstrations of its products and services.

Apple's retail stores feature sleek, minimalist designs, with spacious layouts, abundant natural light, and innovative product displays that invite customers to explore and interact with Apple's latest innovations. In addition to showcasing its products, Apple's stores offer a range of services, including technical support, product workshops, and one-on-one training sessions with Apple experts. By creating welcoming and engaging environments that foster creativity, learning, and community, Apple's retail stores have become destinations in their own right, attracting millions of visitors each year and contributing to the company's brand loyalty and sales growth.

2. Starbucks:

Starbucks, founded by Jerry Baldwin, Zev Siegl, and Gordon Bowker in 1971, has transformed the coffee industry and redefined the concept of the coffee shop as a social gathering place. With over 30,000 stores worldwide, Starbucks has built a global empire based on its commitment to quality, sustainability, and customer experience. While Starbucks offers mobile ordering and drive-thru options, its brick-and-mortar stores remain the heart and soul of its brand, providing customers with a welcoming and comfortable environment to enjoy their favorite coffee beverages.

Starbucks' stores are designed to create a sense of community and connection, with cozy seating areas, free Wi-Fi, and inviting decor that encourages customers to linger and socialize. In addition to its signature coffee beverages, Starbucks' stores offer a range of food options, including pastries, sandwiches, and snacks, as well as branded merchandise and seasonal promotions. By prioritizing customer engagement, employee training, and store ambiance, Starbucks has cultivated a loyal customer base and achieved sustained growth and success in the highly competitive coffee market.

3. IKEA:

IKEA, founded by Ingvar Kamprad in 1943, has revolutionized the furniture industry with its innovative approach to retailing and home furnishings. With over 400 stores in 52 countries, IKEA is known for its sprawling warehouse-style stores, flat-pack furniture designs, and affordable prices. While IKEA also offers online shopping and home delivery options, its brick-and-mortar stores remain the cornerstone of its business model, providing customers with a unique shopping experience that combines inspiration, value, and convenience.

IKEA's stores are designed to showcase its extensive range of furniture and home accessories in real-life room settings, allowing customers to visualize how products will look and function in their own homes. In addition to its showroom floors, IKEA's stores feature restaurants, play areas for children, and other amenities that encourage customers to spend time exploring and interacting with the brand. By offering a seamless shopping experience that combines affordability, quality, and style, IKEA has become a global leader in the furniture industry and a beloved destination for home decor enthusiasts worldwide.

4. Trader Joe's:

Trader Joe's, founded by Joe Coulombe in 1958, has become a cult favorite among food lovers for its unique selection of high-quality, affordable groceries and eclectic store ambiance. With over 500 stores in the United States, Trader Joe's has carved out a niche in the grocery industry by focusing on customer service, product innovation, and a fun, quirky shopping experience. While many grocery chains have embraced online shopping and delivery services, Trader Joe's has remained committed to its brick-and-mortar stores, where customers can discover new products, sample seasonal offerings, and interact with friendly and knowledgeable staff.

Trader Joe's stores are known for their colorful, whimsical decor, with hand-painted murals, quirky signage, and Hawaiian-shirt-clad employees adding to the store's unique charm. In addition to its curated selection of groceries, Trader Joe's offers a range of private-label products that are exclusive to the brand, including gourmet foods, organic produce, and specialty items from around the world. By prioritizing product quality, customer experience, and store ambiance, Trader Joe's has cultivated a fiercely loyal customer base and achieved consistent sales growth and profitability in the competitive grocery market.

Brick-and-mortar businesses continue to thrive and evolve in today's digital age, offering unique experiences, personalized service, and a tangible connection to products and brands. From iconic brands like Apple and Starbucks to innovative retailers like IKEA and Trader Joe's, these real-life examples demonstrate the enduring appeal of brick-and-mortar stores and the importance of customer-centricity, innovation, and community engagement in driving success in the retail industry. By embracing innovation, adapting to changing consumer preferences, and fostering meaningful connections with customers, brick-and-mortar businesses can continue to thrive and remain relevant in the dynamic and competitive retail landscape.

Chapter 7

Resources

Helpful Websites and Online Communities

The internet has become a treasure trove of resources for entrepreneurs and business leaders, offering a wealth of information, tools, and communities to support their ventures. From educational websites and industry-specific platforms to online communities and forums, entrepreneurs have access to a vast array of resources to help them navigate the challenges of starting and growing a business. In this section, we explore some of the most helpful websites and online communities for entrepreneurs seeking guidance, support, and inspiration on their entrepreneurial journey.

1. Entrepreneur.com:

Entrepreneur.com is a leading online resource for entrepreneurs and small business owners, offering a wide range of articles, guides, and resources on topics such as business planning, marketing, finance, and leadership. The website features expert advice from industry professionals, case studies of successful entrepreneurs, and tools and templates to help entrepreneurs launch and grow their businesses. In addition to articles and guides, Entrepreneur.com also hosts webinars, podcasts, and online courses to provide entrepreneurs with actionable insights and practical advice for building successful businesses.

2. Inc.com:

Inc.com is another popular destination for entrepreneurs and business leaders, offering a wealth of articles, videos, and resources on topics such as leadership, innovation, and business strategy. The website features profiles of successful companies and entrepreneurs, as well as insights from industry experts and thought leaders. Inc.com also hosts events, conferences, and webinars to connect entrepreneurs with mentors, investors, and peers, providing valuable networking opportunities and support for business growth.

3. Small Business Administration (SBA):

The Small Business Administration (SBA) is a government agency dedicated to supporting small businesses and entrepreneurs in the United States. The SBA website offers a wealth of resources, including guides on starting and growing a business, information on government programs and resources for small businesses, and access to funding and financing options. Entrepreneurs can also use the SBA website to find local resources, such as Small Business Development Centers (SBDCs) and Women's Business Centers (WBCs), which offer free business counseling, training, and assistance to small business owners.

4. Quora:

Quora is a popular question-and-answer platform where entrepreneurs can ask questions, share knowledge, and connect with industry experts and thought leaders. The platform features a wide range of topics related to entrepreneurship, business development, and industry trends, allowing entrepreneurs to access insights and advice from a diverse community of professionals. Quora also allows users to follow topics and experts, join relevant communities, and participate in discussions to expand their knowledge and network with peers.

5. Reddit - Entrepreneur and Startups Subreddits:

Reddit is a social media platform known for its diverse communities and discussion forums, called subreddits, on a wide range of topics. For entrepreneurs, the Entrepreneur and

Startups subreddits are valuable resources for connecting with like-minded individuals, sharing experiences, and seeking advice and feedback on business ideas and challenges. These subreddits feature discussions on topics such as business planning, marketing strategies, fundraising, and technology trends, providing entrepreneurs with valuable insights and support from the Reddit community.

6. LinkedIn:

LinkedIn is a professional networking platform that offers a range of resources for entrepreneurs and business professionals. In addition to connecting with potential clients, partners, and investors, entrepreneurs can use LinkedIn to access industry news and insights, join relevant groups and communities, and showcase their expertise and accomplishments. LinkedIn also offers a range of educational resources, such as courses, webinars, and articles, to help entrepreneurs develop their skills and stay informed about industry trends and best practices.

7. Meetup:

Meetup is a platform that facilitates in-person and virtual gatherings of people with shared interests and goals. For entrepreneurs, Meetup offers a valuable opportunity to connect with other entrepreneurs, attend networking events, and participate in workshops and seminars on topics such as business development, marketing, and technology. Entrepreneurs can use Meetup to find local events and communities in their area, as well as online events and groups focused on specific industries or interests.

The internet offers a wealth of resources for entrepreneurs and business leaders seeking guidance, support, and inspiration on their entrepreneurial journey. From educational websites and industry-specific platforms to online communities and forums, entrepreneurs have access to a diverse range of resources to help them navigate the challenges of starting and growing a business.

Software Recommendations for Business Management

The right software tools can streamline operations, improve productivity, and enhance decision-making for businesses of all sizes. From project management and accounting to marketing and customer relationship management (CRM), there is a plethora of software options available to help businesses manage various aspects of their operations more efficiently. In this section, we explore some of the top software recommendations for business management across different functional areas.

1. Project Management:

a. **Trello:** Trello is a popular project management tool that uses boards, lists, and cards to organize tasks and workflows. It allows teams to collaborate in real-time, track progress, and prioritize tasks using drag-and-drop functionality. Trello is particularly useful for agile project management, as it offers flexibility and customization to adapt to different project workflows and methodologies.

b. **Asana:** Asana is another widely used project management tool that helps teams organize tasks, assign responsibilities, and track progress towards goals. It offers features such as task dependencies, timelines, and project templates to streamline project planning and execution. Asana also integrates with other popular tools such as Slack, Google Drive, and Microsoft Teams for seamless collaboration and communication.

c. **Jira:** Jira is a project management tool designed for software development teams, offering features such as issue tracking, agile boards, and release planning. It allows teams to plan and track work using agile methodologies such as Scrum and Kanban, with customizable workflows and reporting capabilities. Jira integrates with popular development tools such as GitHub and Bitbucket for end-to-end software development lifecycle management.

2. Accounting and Financial Management:

a. **QuickBooks:** QuickBooks is a leading accounting software solution for small and medium-sized businesses, offering features such as invoicing, expense tracking, and financial reporting. It allows businesses to manage their finances more efficiently, automate repetitive tasks, and gain insights into their financial performance. QuickBooks also integrates with other business tools such as PayPal, Shopify, and Square for seamless transaction management.

b. **Xero:** Xero is another popular accounting software solution that offers similar features to QuickBooks, with a focus on simplicity and ease of use. It allows businesses to manage invoicing, bank reconciliation, and payroll processing from a single platform. Xero also offers advanced features such as multi-currency support, inventory tracking, and budgeting tools to help businesses stay on top of their finances.

c. **FreshBooks:** FreshBooks is a cloud-based accounting software solution designed for freelancers and small businesses, offering features such as time tracking, project management, and client invoicing. It allows users to create professional-looking invoices, track expenses, and accept online payments, making it easier to manage finances and cash flow. FreshBooks also integrates with other popular business tools such as Stripe, PayPal, and G Suite for added convenience.

3. Marketing and Sales:

a. **HubSpot:** HubSpot is an all-in-one marketing and sales software platform that helps businesses attract, engage, and delight customers at every stage of the buyer's journey. It offers features such as email marketing, lead generation, social media management, and customer relationship management (CRM) in one integrated platform. HubSpot also provides analytics and reporting tools to track marketing ROI and sales performance.

b. **Mailchimp:** Mailchimp is a popular email marketing platform that helps businesses create, send, and track email campaigns to engage with their audience and drive sales. It offers features such as email automation, audience segmentation, and A/B testing to optimize campaign performance. Mailchimp also integrates with other marketing tools such as Shopify, WordPress, and Facebook for seamless campaign management.

c. **Salesforce:** Salesforce is a cloud-based CRM platform that helps businesses manage customer relationships, sales pipelines, and marketing campaigns in one centralized platform. It offers features such as lead management, opportunity tracking, and sales forecasting to help businesses close deals and drive revenue growth. Salesforce also provides advanced analytics and AI-powered insights to help businesses personalize customer interactions and drive engagement.

4. Human Resources and Employee Management:

a. **BambooHR:** BambooHR is a human resources management software solution that helps businesses manage employee data, track time off, and streamline HR processes such as recruiting and onboarding. It offers features such as employee self-service, performance management, and compliance tracking to help businesses effectively manage their workforce. BambooHR also integrates with other HR tools such as Paylocity, ADP, and Greenhouse for seamless data integration.

b. **Gusto:** Gusto is a cloud-based payroll and HR platform designed for small businesses, offering features such as payroll processing, benefits administration, and HR compliance. It allows businesses to automate payroll calculations, manage employee benefits, and stay compliant with state and federal regulations. Gusto also offers HR advisory services and support to help businesses navigate complex HR issues.

c. **Zenefits:** Zenefits is an all-in-one HR platform that combines payroll, benefits, and compliance management in one integrated solution. It offers features such as automated onboarding, time tracking, and employee performance management to help businesses streamline HR processes and improve employee engagement. Zenefits also provides access to a network of HR professionals and experts for additional support and guidance.

The right software tools can make a significant difference in streamlining operations, improving productivity, and enhancing decision-making for businesses of all sizes. From project management and accounting to marketing and human resources, there are a plethora of software options available to help businesses manage various aspects of their operations more efficiently. By leveraging these software recommendations effectively, businesses can optimize their workflows, drive growth, and achieve greater success in today's competitive business landscape.

Industry Reports and Market Analysis Sources

In the fast-paced and ever-evolving world of business, staying informed about industry trends, market dynamics, and competitive landscapes is essential for making informed decisions and driving strategic growth. Industry reports and market analysis sources provide valuable insights and data-driven intelligence to help entrepreneurs and business leaders understand market trends, identify opportunities, and mitigate risks. In this section, we explore some of the most reputable sources for industry reports and market analysis, offering a comprehensive guide for accessing the information needed to stay ahead in today's competitive business environment.

1. MarketResearch.com:

MarketResearch.com is a leading provider of market research reports and industry analysis, offering a vast repository of reports covering a wide range of industries and sectors. The platform features reports from reputable market research firms and analysts, providing in-depth insights into market trends, consumer behavior, competitive landscapes, and emerging opportunities. MarketResearch.com also offers custom research services, allowing businesses to commission tailored reports and analysis to meet their specific needs.

2. IBISWorld:

IBISWorld is a trusted source for industry research and analysis, offering comprehensive reports on thousands of industries across the globe. The platform provides detailed insights into market size, growth trends, competitive dynamics, and key success factors, helping businesses make informed decisions and develop effective strategies. IBISWorld's reports are widely used by entrepreneurs, investors, and industry professionals to assess market opportunities, evaluate competitive threats, and identify growth prospects.

3. Statista:

Statista is a leading provider of statistical data and market research, offering access to a vast database of industry reports, charts, and infographics. The platform covers a wide range of industries and topics, including technology, finance, healthcare, and consumer goods, providing users with valuable insights and analysis to inform their decision-making processes. Statista's reports are trusted by businesses, researchers, and policymakers worldwide for their accuracy, reliability, and depth of coverage.

4. Euromonitor International:

Euromonitor International is a global market research company that provides strategic intelligence on consumer markets, industries, and trends. The platform offers a range of reports and databases covering various sectors, including consumer goods, retailing, travel, and technology. Euromonitor International's reports are renowned for their comprehensive coverage, rigorous methodology, and actionable insights, making them a valuable resource for businesses seeking to understand market dynamics and capitalize on emerging opportunities.

5. Deloitte Insights:

Deloitte Insights is a platform that provides thought leadership, analysis, and research from Deloitte's global network of experts. The platform offers a wide range of industry reports, white papers, and insights on topics such as technology, finance, healthcare, and consumer trends. Deloitte Insights' reports are highly regarded for their depth of analysis, strategic insights, and actionable recommendations, making them a valuable resource for businesses seeking to navigate complex market dynamics and drive growth.

6. Gartner:

Gartner is a leading research and advisory company that provides insights, analysis, and advice on a wide range of technology-related topics. The platform offers research reports, market forecasts, and strategic guidance on emerging technologies, IT trends, and digital transformation initiatives. Gartner's reports are widely used by businesses, IT professionals, and industry leaders to assess market opportunities, evaluate technology vendors, and make informed decisions about technology investments and strategies.

7. Forrester Research:

Forrester Research is a research and advisory firm that provides insights and analysis on technology, marketing, and customer experience trends. The platform offers research reports, data-driven insights, and strategic guidance to help businesses navigate digital disruption, drive innovation, and enhance customer engagement. Forrester Research's reports are trusted by businesses, marketers, and CX professionals for their depth of analysis, actionable recommendations, and thought leadership in the industry.

Industry reports and market analysis sources are valuable resources for entrepreneurs and business leaders seeking to gain insights into market trends, competitive dynamics, and emerging opportunities. Whether it's accessing reports from reputable market research firms like MarketResearch.com and IBISWorld, or leveraging insights from platforms like Statista and Euromonitor International, businesses can use these resources to inform their strategic decision-making processes and drive growth in today's competitive business landscape. By staying informed about industry trends and market dynamics, businesses can identify new opportunities, mitigate risks, and stay ahead of the competition in an ever-changing business environment.

Conclusion

As we reach the conclusion of this book, it's clear that the landscape of entrepreneurship and business is evolving at an unprecedented pace. From the rise of remote work and sustainability initiatives to the rapid advancement of technology, the challenges and opportunities facing entrepreneurs today are diverse and dynamic. Throughout this guide, we've explored various aspects of modern business, from identifying strengths and interests to building successful ventures and adapting to future trends.

At the heart of this guide lies the recognition that entrepreneurship is a journey filled with both triumphs and trials. It requires resilience, creativity, and a willingness to embrace change. By identifying our strengths and interests, we can align our passions with profitable business opportunities, setting the stage for success. From low-investment ventures to tech-driven startups and brick-and-mortar establishments, the possibilities are endless for those willing to pursue their entrepreneurial dreams.

Moreover, building a successful business requires more than just a great idea; it requires careful planning, strategic execution, and a commitment to continuous improvement. Crafting a solid business plan, understanding your target audience, and leveraging technology and online tools are essential components of building a strong foundation for your venture. By focusing on building a strong brand, establishing a strong online presence, and embracing innovation, entrepreneurs can position their businesses for long-term success in a rapidly changing world.

As we look to the future of work and business, it's clear that adaptation and agility will be key to staying competitive and thriving in an ever-evolving landscape. By embracing change, seizing opportunities, and leveraging the resources available to us, we can navigate the challenges ahead and build businesses that not only survive but thrive in the years to come.

In closing, this book is a testament to the spirit of entrepreneurship and the boundless potential of human ingenuity. Whether you're a seasoned entrepreneur or just starting on your journey, I hope this guide has provided you with valuable insights, inspiration, and practical strategies for achieving success in the dynamic world of modern business. Remember, the future belongs to those who dare to dream, innovate, and take bold action. Here's to your success in business and beyond.

Dear Reader,

I hope you found the book insightful and valuable.

Your feedback is invaluable to me. If you enjoyed reading this book, I would appreciate it if you could take a moment to leave a review on the reading apps and platforms.

Thank you for your support, and I wish you all the best.

Kind regards,
Ghazwan

About the Author

Ghazwan is a passionate entrepreneur and business strategist dedicated to helping individuals and organizations achieve their full potential with a deep understanding of modern businesses' challenges and opportunities.

With a Master's degree in Computer and Systems Sciences from Stockholm University, specializing in eService design, requirement engineering, and business process management, he is equipped to innovate cutting-edge solutions.

He believes in the power of collaboration and lifelong learning, and his mission is to empower people to reach their goals and positively impact the world.